10 Financial Tips for You and Your Family

Unless you HATE your Family.

Michael Nunneley

Copyright © 2018 by Michael Nunneley & Family Wild, LLC

All rights reserved. No part of this publication may be reproduced, distributed, or transmitted in any form or by any means, including photocopying, recording, or other electronic or mechanical methods, without the prior written permission of the publisher, except in the case of brief quotations embodied in critical reviews and certain other noncommercial uses permitted by copyright law. For permission requests, email to the publisher, addressed "Attention: Permissions Coordinator," at the email address below.

Family Wild, LLC
Email address: universalbankingu@gmail.com
Website: www.universalbankingu.com
Facebook —
https://www.facebook.com/Familywild2016/

Family Wild Online Store -https://squareup.com/store/familyenterprisein.com

The information provided within this Book is for general informational purposes only. While we try to keep the information up - to - date and correct, there are no representations or warranties, express or implied, about the completeness, accuracy, reliability, suitability or availability with respect to the information, products, services, or related graphics contained in this Book for any purpose. Any use of this information is at your own risk and the risk of your friends and family.

The information contained within this Book is strictly for educational purposes. If you wish to apply ideas contained in this Book, you are taking full responsibility for your actions.

2nd Edition
ISBN - 13: 9781728919287

Cover Illustration Copyright © 2017 M W Nunneley
Cover design by M.W. Nunneley
Editing by Kim Nunneley, Marilyn Beyer, Del Beyer, Nick Baird, J. M. Nunneley

Other books by Michael Nunneley

Fishing for a Business Loan

A Banker's Magic Bean

The Family Wild Fishing Handbook

The Family Wild Art Handbook — **by Kim Beyer (Mike's Wife)**

The Family Wild Hunting Activities Manual — Volume I

The Family Wild Fishing Activities Manual — Volume I

The Family Wild Art Activities Manual — Volume I — **by Kim Beyer (Mike's Wife)**

The Family Wild Video/Photography Manual — Volume I

For Kim—

Take my advice folks - talk to your spouse about your finances - it's a team sport.

"You Can't Stop Stupid,
You Can't Cure Crazy, and
You Can't Teach Happy."

-Michael Nunneley

Acknowledgements

Kim Nunneley -my BEST Friend, my Wife, my Teacher,
my Pillow Pal.

My Parents Wes & Karen - for providing me
a family business experience.

Del & Marilyn, Brian, Kristi & Bryce-for their support –
in good times and bad.

Our Nunneley Family -
for their patience with their Parents/Grandparents
**Ashley, Michael, Nathan & Will, Joshua & Sarah, Courtney,
Robbie, Ashley, Gabe & Izzy, & Ian**

My Brother Tim - we failed at business together -but earned a
Master's Degree in business at the School of Hard Knocks.
My Sister Sue – who recognized early
when to stay and when to leave.

Larry and Pam Howison – our friends and my big brother & sister.

David Morrison, a banker who took a chance on a Central Michigan
University Grad who could add and subtract, multiply and divide.

Donna - my dear friend who helped me prove a couple of Northern
Michigan chubby kids could succeed in the corporate banking
environment and earned the wisdom to get the hell out of it.

The DAWGS -who taught me a lifetime of guy friendship.

All the businesses and individuals I've worked with in banking –
I always strived to tell you ***the Good, the Bad & the Ugly***
as a banker and as a person.

Table of Contents

Introduction   11

Chapter 1 - Debt - Want vs. Need   13

If you are pondering a personal loan - stop and consider this chapter before you sign the dotted line. Don't dig the debt hole deeper unless you absolutely need, for survival, borrowed money.

Chapter 2 - Your Credit Report   19

Do you understand the importance of your credit report? If not, you should. Consider why you should passionately monitor your credit report and identity.

Chapter 3 - Pyramids & Trees - Get out of Debt   27

Are you paying your bills wrong? What if I told you the way you pay your bills can reduce your debt faster and without having to get another job, sell a pint of blood or buy lottery tickets - and with the money you already use to pay your bills.

Chapter 4 - Applying for a Loan   47

You've decided to pursue a loan, now what? How can you prepare yourself for the loan process? Learn how to save yourself time, effort and potential grief - before you apply for a loan.

Chapter 5 - Co-signing a Loan   59

Your child, grandchild, niece, nephew, friend has asked you to "just" co-sign a loan with them. What does that really mean? More important, what happens to you and your credit if your loving family member/friend defaults on their loan.

Chapter 6 - Titles on Financial Accounts   66

Does it matter who you put on your checking account? Only if you care who can access your money, make changes on the account and ultimately close your account. On the other hand, consider something worse - if you're the only person titled on your account.

Chapter 7 - Power of Attorney 71
Instead of dying, can your relatives access your financial accounts if you (and your spouse) are in an accident and are unable to handle your finances? Who will pay your bills? How can you protect your finances without adding someone as an owner of your accounts?

Chapter 8 - Beneficiary's/POD/ITF 75
Imagine you died - TODAY. Would your survivors be able to access your money? Not sure? This chapter will decide if you hate your family.

Chapter 9 - Last Wills & Testament 83
Ok, so you're still dead again. If you don't have a will, you HATE your family. If you have a will, does that mean your relatives can access your accounts? NO. Understand the importance of creating a will.

Chapter 10 - Trusts 89
What is a trust? Do I need one? I thought only rich people needed trusts. How can establishing a trust protect me, my assets and show my family my love?

Conclusion - Give a Gift 97
Ask yourself if anyone you know and love could use this book when you're done? If you want to keep your copy - would this make a more impactful Christmas gift than an ugly holiday sweater or fruit cake?

Appendix - 99

About the Author 105

Introduction
I didn't grow up dreaming of being a banker. No one does.

I want you to know I've made **EVERY MISTAKE** financially you can make. I'm still suffering financially, as are my children, my wife (who has made her share of financial mistakes), my ex - wife (as our financial decisions led in some part to that event) and my grandchildren.

I need you to know why I've written this book: so, you don't make the same mistakes I've made and so you don't suffer the consequences I've suffered and continue to shoulder.

If you've made it this far, let's get started with the Good, the Bad, the Ugly of

-

10 Financial Tips for You and Your Family

Unless you HATE your Family.

Chapter 1

DEBT
Want vs. Need

> The real question –
> ## *Do I (we) need this loan?*

> I've yet to find a Banker who ever asked customers this question: "Do you want or do you need this loan/debt?"
> *Can you imagine a used car salesman asking you the same question?*

If you both answered you NEED a loan, then proceed. If you answer you WANT this loan but you really don't NEED this loan for a vital and critical purpose such as shelter or necessary transportation, then I urge you to

STOP.

Wait a week, then ask yourself, "can I live without this new debt?" If you don't pursue a loan, will you cease to exist, will you live in a cardboard box, will you have to borrow the neighbor kid's bike to get to work?

I beg you - never apply for a loan you don't absolutely need. Let's see why.

Before you walk into a credit union or bank, you need to decide for yourself whether you would loan yourself this amount of money given your financial situation. **WHY???**

> ## Knowing your own financial situation, Would YOU loan Yourself the Money?

If you do decide to pursue a loan, in my books *Fishing for a Personal Loan* and *Fishing for a Business Loan*, I highlight RED FLAG thoughts and questions bankers consider when reviewing a loan request. First and foremost, when you walk into my office, I want to understand how well *"You"* know your own finances. If you don't have a grasp of how money comes in and goes out of your household, how in the world will you pay off your loan? Will you hope for the best? Pray? Maybe rely on dumb luck?

Ask yourself "Do I have or even understand a budget?" If you answer no to either, you need to invest time and energy into learning how to create, monitor and live on a budget to maximize your personal and business cash flow.

Everyday people "fish" for loans or refinancing because they don't want to take control of their finances. "I just need a loan to get through the next couple months" or "I just want to refinance things to help with my bills." If this sounds familiar, ask yourself, "do I understand how every dollar comes into and goes out of my life?"

Do you review your existing loans, credit card bills, power, heat, insurance, car payments, and home mortgage statements? Do you really know where every dollar goes? How about how much you spend on coffee, restaurants, and other non - necessities?

I used to own a photography business. Many wonderful photographers opened their business and created much visually "better" portraits than I ever did but they didn't last two years - why? Because they LOVED taking pictures and HATED the business aspects of owning and operating a studio and since they HATED it, they didn't do it.

If you don't devote at least a couple hours a week tracking your money, you'll work two or three times as hard as you need to just to make ends meet simply because you're not watching your cash and ultimately making accurate decisions.

Do you balance your checkbook(s) monthly?

IF the answer is no because banks never make mistakes, the online banking does it for me, or it's close enough, I want to ask you if you were SOUND ASLEEP during the Great Recession of 2008.

Banks make mistakes, sometimes BIG ones and sometimes small ones (*small ones add up to big ones*). If there was a dollar on the ground, would you pick it up? If so, then why wouldn't you balance your own checkbook?

I paid a professional business advisor, Charles Lewis, thousands of dollars and he taught me:

Successful people do the things that the failures won't do.

Which is primarily the financial part of life. It's not fun. In fact, it's **AWFUL,** until you go to the bank to check your deposit balances... By the way, bankers love deposits. Deposits pay back your loans.

Balancing your finances doesn't end with checking and/or savings accounts. You need to take a few moments and "balance" your credit card statements, your car loans, your home mortgages, and your other loans. If you have retirement investments, make sure you don't just open the envelope, file the report, and throw out the empty envelope without looking at how your finances are performing.

If you don't meet at least annually with your financial advisor, you have a problem. If you happen to have a great advisor, you may love seeing your financial results. However, in a down market, you may not enjoy looking at your report, but you'll stay on top of YOUR investments.

You're not staying on top of your investments and worse, your advisor isn't either or they would have called you in recent memory. Call them, today, and review your retirement **ASS**ets (not a typo).

In my books, *Fishing for a Business Loan* and *Fishing for a Personal Loan*, I offer you a summary of highlights at the end of each chapter called *Tackle this Box*.

Since I love fishing and the theme still works, I've included the things you need to tackle to ensure your financial tackle box is in order. Most important, do these things before you try and borrow any money. Until you get your financial house in order, you have no business going deeper into debt.

You have to TACKLE this BOX

____ Do You Want or **NEED** a loan/your debt?
____ Do you have a personal budget that tracks every dollar coming into your life and going out?
____ Do you have a savings account/plan for emergencies?
____ Do you balance your checkbook monthly?
____ Do you balance/review your loan statements monthly?
____ Do you balance/review your credit card statements monthly?
____ Do you have a retirement plan?
____ Do you review your monthly retirement/investment statement every month?

TACKLE THIS NOW.

Chapter 2

Your Credit Report

Why should you pull your credit report and where?

Protect your credit like you would protect your children.

Truth be told, I wouldn't go into business or into a relationship without knowing a partner's credit history and score. Banks, credit unions, insurance agencies, employment agencies, and landlords require those reports for a reason.

If you want to impress your banker, hand them your free credit report and prove you know you have a 717 - credit score. Most bankers will try and help you improve your credit scores if you prove you understand where your credit score stands.

Imagine the student who never goes to the teacher to ask for extra help versus the student who invests extra time with the teacher, with a tutor and in study hall. Which student will earn the benefit of the doubt and who's grade will reflect the effort or lack thereof?

Regardless of your credit score, I recommend you monitor it regularly. Be careful. There are many credit reporting entities. Some are legitimate and others not so much.

Personally, I use **annualcreditreport.com.** I also use the phone app **Credit Karma**. You can get a free copy of your credit report that will show your debts, public information and your payment history, but won't show your score unless you pay a nominal fee for it. You can receive a free credit report from multiple sources, which may include some of your existing credit cards.

Why would you do this? Your credit score impacts the interest rate on your loans and credit cards. Did you know your credit score can dramatically impact your home insurance, car insurances, life insurance, and health insurances rates?

Also, many landlords require a credit report just to qualify you as a renter. If you want to save yourself hundreds if not thousands of dollars, know and protect your personal credit score.

Everyone faces the reality of Identity theft and credit fraud. Literally with the push of a wrong button on a social security number or with the outright theft of financial information, you can expect to spend hours and hours trying to repair your credit history.

Don't believe me. Just ask a couple friends if they've ever heard of anyone victimized by identity theft. It won't take long to find one. Then ask them how long it took them to resolve the issue and ask if they wish they'd done a better job monitoring their personal credit.

So, what? People get loans everyday with bad credit, right? It says so on the internet and you can believe everything on the internet, correct? I hope you have a credit score of 700 or higher *and you know it*. If so, read on, laugh, and enjoy as you continue to protect that number.

For those not laughing, denied for a loan or credit card, lost out renting an apartment, or paid higher rates on car or life insurance, you may want to take notes on this section.

Let's say you applied for a loan and according to your banker, she can't lend to you with a 548 - credit score. You had an uneasy feeling about your credit score, but you didn't know your credit score was this bad **(most people don't)**.

So now, right now, make your plan. Seriously, do **YOU** feel smarter today? You should. You just confirmed that you have a credit issue. You may receive a copy of your credit report from the bank or credit union or you may not. If you don't, **order it TODAY**. If you don't know how to read it, GOOGLE "How to read your credit report." Better yet, call your banker and have him or her review it with you. Once you've studied your credit report and understand what caused your score, I want you to head to EGYPT. Ok, just Google pyramid because I want you to see a visual representation of how to "rebuild" your credit.

Then, I want you to put your credit issues/debts *in order from smallest to largest by total amount – think pyramid*. In addition, I want you to list out the payments and I want you to find the interest rates for all credit on your statements. Again, if you don't know how to read a credit card, loan or mortgage statement, ask your banker.

At this point, your banker will brag to anyone who'll listen about how one of their clients actually took ownership and blame of their financial decline in order to improve their credit score and financial well - being. (Don't worry, we can't use your real name or we'll get fired).

Let's look at a scenario. Remember this represents "your" personal debt picture.

Table 1

Your Debt	Amount	Minimum Payment	Actual Payment	Interest Rate
Mortgage	$ 50,000	$ 400	$ 500	4.50%
Car	$ 20,000	$ 265	$ 265	3.00%
LOC	$ 10,000	$ 50	$ 100	4.75%
Credit Card #1	$ 1,000	$ 25	$ 50	2.90%
Credit Card #2	$ 3,000	$ 50	$ 75	9.99%
Credit Card #3	$ 6,000	$ 100	$ 100	19.99%

Your credit report shows you also have two medical bills on your credit report that are in collection, one for $200 and the other for $1000 from when you had your appendix removed three years ago.

You also got behind on your credit cards when things got tight a couple months ago, because of Christmas and your vacation.
(You went on vacation with a 548 - credit score???)

You have delinquent property taxes of $400 on your home.
(Really? You went on vacation?)

Finally, all in one place and in black and white - all of your current credit staring you in the face. Where do you start? First of all, you have to determine what issue *most negatively affects* your credit score as describe above.

You need to think like a banker. What scares a banker more than anything?

Government.

Your tax issues sit atop your credit pyramid like a star on a Christmas Tree. Like I just said, governments scare banks and kill credit scores. As a result, what should you tackle first?

Your two collections come in right behind your tax issue. Again, banks hate collections more than an occasional late payment on a debt. Why? Because this means you've totally given up paying on a debt you owe and we view that as much worse than "just" a late payment.

In the next chapter, we'll cover the next steps on your road to becoming debt free and improving your credit score. However, in short, do whatever you can to pay off your tax lien, charge-offs and bring your other debts current and paid as agreed.

Addressing these issues will improve your credit score as long as you pay everything on time, every time, all the time moving forward.

However, you'll continue your miserable debt existence if you keep charging on your credit cards and drawing from your line of credit. If you truly want to control your debt, you need to pay in cash or with a check and only spend what you budget.

Do not close/cancel your credit cards or lines.

> Once you decide to not actively use your credit cards or lines of credit, you need to place your cards in your files, your safety deposit box, freeze them in a block of ice, but don't close or cancel them.

The credit agencies use a variety of algorithms to determine your score. One of the main calculations involves how much debt you have versus how much you have available on your credit cards/lines. If you close a credit card that has no remaining debt, you, in effect, make this calculation worse.

Closing your credit cards/lines will have a negative effect on your credit score. As a result, just make them unavailable to yourself. In other words, don't add more debt to your pyramid.

 ## You have to TACKLE this BOX

____ Pull your Free Annual Credit report from a reputable reporting agency. I use **annualcreditreport.com**, however do your own research to find the report that best suits you.

____ Consider signing up for a credit monitoring app like **Credit Karma**. Again, do your own research to find the report that best suits you.

____ Review the credit weaknesses on the report.

____ Go through each bill listed and confirm your past & present obligations.

____ If you find something you don't recognize or believe inaccurate, contact the business (i.e. credit card company, bank, phone company) **immediately** and dispute. You can typically find their contact information within the report. If not, or if you don't recognize it, look it up on the Web based on the title. Continue your dispute until can no longer find it on your credit report. *Demand a letter or other documentation as proof of final resolution.*

____ If you find wrong information on the report also contact the reporting agency to dispute it.

____ At the very least, pull your free credit reports **annually**. Put this on your calendar or in your phone to remind you.

____ Consider buying into a reputable credit report and credit notification service, **annualcreditreport.com** for example**,** to let you know immediately if something has changed on your credit report.

____ Protect your credit score, every second of every minute of every hour of every day.

Chapter 3

Pyramids and Trees

> How to Improve your
> # Credit Score
> and CHOP Down Debt

If you have debt, how do you make your payments? Do you pay off each of your debts on time, every time, all the time?

Do you have long term debt for a car or a house? Do you put extra on some/each of your debt payments? Most people tend to follow this plan.

What if I told you there's a better way to pay your bills?

I'd like to use the following scenario to illustrate my suggestion. Let's say you have the following debts:

Table 2

Your Debt	Amount	Minimum Payment	Actual Payment	Interest Rate
Credit Card #3	$ 6,000	$ 100	$ 100	19.99%
Credit Card #2	$ 3,000	$ 50	$ 75	9.99%
LOC	$ 10,000	$ 50	$ 100	4.75%
Mortgage	$ 50,000	$ 400	$ 500	4.50%
Car	$ 20,000	$ 265	$ 265	3.00%
Credit Card #1	$ 1,000	$ 25	$ 50	2.90%
Med Col #2	$ 1,000	$ -	$ -	Late Fee
Tax Lien	$ 400	$ -	$ -	Varies
Med Col #1	$ 400	$ -	$ -	Late Fee
Total	$ 91,800	$ 890	$ 1,090	7.54%

This scenario should cover some of the typical bills facing today's families. In fact, most would consider this as a worst-case scenario. Our family appears to have planted themselves a deep debt forest.

Note - Tax Liens and Accounts in Collection absolutely decimate your credit score. No matter what the circumstances, you want to pay these off as soon as possible

As you can see, they're actually paying a bit extra on a couple of their debts - $200 a month in total. As mentioned, this reflects a typical family debt forest.

What if I told you that you could pay down your debt faster and save thousands of dollars in interest just by changing how you allocate your current "extra" payment resources?

Remember, I want to make sure you still get to eat (check out my picture. I like to eat). Further, since I don't have the magic bean for a money tree, we have to use the money our example family (you) currently uses to pay their bills. Remember you owe:

Table 3

Your Debt	Amount	Minimum Payment	Actual Payment	Interest Rate
Credit Card #3	$ 6,000	$ 100	$ 100	19.99%
Credit Card #2	$ 3,000	$ 50	$ 75	9.99%
LOC	$ 10,000	$ 50	$ 100	4.75%
Mortgage	$ 50,000	$ 400	$ 500	4.50%
Car	$ 20,000	$ 265	$ 265	3.00%
Credit Card #1	$ 1,000	$ 25	$ 50	2.90%
Med Col #2	$ 1,000	$ -	$ -	Late Fee
Tax Lien	$ 400	$ -	$ -	Varies
Med Col #1	$ 400	$ -	$ -	Late Fee
Total	$ 91,800	$ 890	$ 1,090	7.54%

If you look at what you're paying in our scenario, you're actually shelling out $200 extra on your bills. I told you we wouldn't change how you eat, so you have $200 a month extra to use to pay down debt without having to get another job, finding a better paying job, getting full time work, or selling a pint of blood.

Let's get started.

What do you perceive as the most important debt in your forest? Based on the way you're making your payments, your Mortgage, Line of Credit and Credit Card #2 appear to be your most critical debts as you chose to pay them off quicker by adding to their required minimum payments.

Why do you think someone would make the extra payments as they have in our example?

How do you currently pay your bills? Why? Have you ever considered prioritizing your extra payments based on the importance of your debts to your credit score and your debt forest?

So, let's revisit your debt and how long it will take you to pay it off your way.

As a banker, I'm terrible with numbers (that's my only banker joke). So, I put them on paper and actually look at them to draft a plan. The following will show you about how many payments it will take you to pay off your loans as described above the way "you" (our example borrower) pay them off.

If you own a mortgage balance of $50,000 at 4.5% interest, and you make a $500 monthly payment, you have approximately **168 payments** remaining on your mortgage by paying extra - nice, right???

On your Home Equity Line of Credit at the payments you're making, it will take you about **127 Months** to pay off your LOC. This may actually end up longer as many Home Equity lines use interest only minimum payments *AND* you can borrow more money as you pay it down, so does it ever really go away?

On Credit Card #1, it will take about **20 months** to pay off completely at the rate we're going.

At your current payment, you will eliminate Credit Card #2 in about **48 months** at a $100 a month payment.

Sit down for Credit Card #3. If you make a $100 payment on this card, you will pay for the next **247 months** on that Big Mac, movie rental, new shirt, and vacation you used Credit Card #3 for payment (but you *did* earn all those POINTS by using it - enjoy that $25.00 Gift Card).
As for your car, you have nearly **84 months** of payments to make before you own the car (instead of your bank).
Let's summarize. It will take between 21 months - 247 months to pay off each of your individual debts.

CUTTING DOWN TREES/IMPROVING YOUR CREDIT

Imagine trying to cut down a forest by taking tiny weeny bites out of a bunch of trees. Do you see the similarity between this and your debt payment strategy? Let's try it my way. GRAB YOUR AXE, LUMBERJACK... We'll take the same scenario, but you'll climb out of debt faster AND you won't have to come up with one extra dollar. We'll just move things around a bit, create a plan and stick to the plan. Why?

> # Because HOPE isn't a plan.

Let's review **ALL** your debt including your two medical collections and the tax lien on your credit report.

Table 4

Your Debt	Amount	Minimum Payment	Actual Payment	Interest Rate
Credit Card #3	$ 6,000	$ 100	$ 100	19.99%
Credit Card #2	$ 3,000	$ 50	$ 75	9.99%
LOC	$ 10,000	$ 50	$ 100	4.75%
Mortgage	$ 50,000	$ 400	$ 500	4.50%
Car	$ 20,000	$ 265	$ 265	3.00%
Credit Card #1	$ 1,000	$ 25	$ 50	2.90%
Med Col #2	$ 1,000	$ -	$ -	Late Fee
Tax Lien	$ 400	$ -	$ -	Varies
Med Col #1	$ 400	$ -	$ -	Late Fee
Total	$ 91,800	$ 890	$ 1,090	7.54%

The First Thing you NEED to do is list ALL YOUR DEBTS out like above.

Now you can see it in all its glory - YOUR DEBT FOREST. Now, how about you fire up that saw and start cutting down some debt trees.

I want to take a moment and congratulate you. Seriously, IF you've taken the time to lay all your debt out and put it in a spreadsheet so you can "see" ALL of it, you've exceeded the norm.

> Now, I want you to put your debt in order from the lowest total down to the highest total - like a pyramid

Table 5

Your Debt	Amount	Minimum Payment	Actual Payment	Interest Rate
Medical #1	$ 200	?		Late Fee
Tax Lien	$ 400	?		Varies
Medical #2	$ 1,000	?		Late Fee
Credit Card #1	$ 1,000	$ 25		2.99%
Credit Card #2	$ 3,000	$ 50		9.99%
Credit Card #3	$ 6,000	$ 100		19.99%
LOC	$ 10,000	$ 100		4.75%
Car	$ 20,000	$ 265		3.00%
Mortgage	$ 50,000	$ 400		4.50%
Total	$ 91,600	$ 940	$ -	7.54%

You've just taken GIANT STEP NUMBER TWO on the road to your financial recovery.

BONUS STEP - I recommend you print off your debt and put it next to your bathroom mirror, over your dresser, above your tooth brush, or anywhere you have to look at it every day. Update it monthly and the moment you pay off a debt so it never leaves your mind's eye.

This will dramatically encourage you to take your bonus money, cash from bottle/can returnables, change from the couch, dollars you found in the wash and apply them all to your debt - which chops it down faster!

Find a FREE blank copy of this on our website at
universalbankingu.com

Remember, you currently pay a total of $200 extra a month. If you can come up with even more cash by selling things, not eating out, not going to the movies, etc. you'll chop your debt forest down quicker. For our purpose, we'll just use the $200 a month you currently pay extra on all your debts.

Outstanding tax liens kill a credit score and scare bankers. If you take that extra $200 a month we just mentioned, you can pay off your tax lien in just two months, resulting in an instant improvement in your credit score (once the credit bureaus record it).

Remember, you haven't tried to find new money to accomplish this. All you've done is move the "extra" money you paid on your mortgage, credit card and line of credit and redirected it to pay off your tax lien. Since you only used your "extra" money, you accomplished this without changing how you eat.

In addition, you made the minimum payments on all of your other debts, on time and every time. Do you know what bankers love - minimum payments, on time, every time. You'll never hear a complaint or see your credit score drop if you make your minimum payment on time, every time.

Let's take a look at the next thing on your Debt Pyramid – your two collections. If you have a legitimate reason for not paying them, you need to make sure you have documentation for your banker explaining the issue and to send to the credit bureaus to dispute these charge - offs.

HEY. You have to do this because until you spend hours mailing the credit bureaus documentation, calling them back, bugging them, threatening them with a call from your lawyer until they send you confirmation that these were actually incorrectly reported on your credit bureau, guess what? They stay on your report.

So, if you have a legitimate credit bureau dispute, attack it until you've killed it and then confirm its removal from your credit report. Also, remember, we only used the "extra" money you already pay on your debts. If you had a garage sale, sold the Nordic Track you thought you'd use but never did, quit going out to dinner two nights a week, quit spending $10 a day for lunch five days a week in addition to grabbing a second job on the weekends, you can cut these debt trees down faster.

- How soon do you want this behind you?
- How soon do you want your credit score to improve?
- How soon do you want a loan?
- What are you willing to change to make all of this happen?
- Who ultimately decides how quickly you get out of debt and improve your credit score.

Next, we actually come to the exciting part. You get to become a LUMBERJACK. **A LUMBERJACK???** Stay with me.

Months #1 thru #2 - Instead of paying a little bit extra on three debts, you will pay all of your extra on one debt. First, you will pay your extra $200 a month for the next two months on your Tax Lien and SHAZAM - you've paid off your Tax Lien. Great job, you've chopped down a HUGE debt tree.

Month #3 - Take your entire extra payment amount and pay off Medical Bill #1 in full for $200. As for all your other bills, you will always pay the minimum payment on time, all the time, every time. Remember to ask for a receipt or a paid in full notice of this collection. Further, you'll need to watch your credit report for this collection to reflect **"Paid."**

Months #4 thru #8 -Take your same extra $200 and pay off your second Medical Collection. In less than a year, you've paid off the three Debt Trees that most negatively affect your credit score. You did this while paying your other bills as agreed, and you've done this without affecting the quality of the food you can buy.

Months #9 thru #12 - Smile, now comes the fun part. Now you get to actually CUT into your normal debt. Take that extra $200 you used to pay down your taxes and collections and **add it to the minimum payment of your lowest credit card, Card #2, of $1,000**.

You need to add all of it and don't spread it out to other debt or worse – spend it.

If you take the $200 a month plus the minimum $25 monthly payment, less what you've paid down, it will take you four more months to pay off this credit card.

> ***In one year, you've taken control of your finances and paid off 4 debts in full.***

*Note - for the purposes of this exercise, I've rounded up the annual Net Amounts to the nearest $25.00 to help simplify this analysis.

High Five & Belly Bump

After Year One.

Table 6

Your Debt	Amount	Minimum Payment	Actual Payment	Interest Rate	Months to Pay Off
Medical #1		Paid In Full !!!			1
Tax Lien		Paid In Full !!!			3
Medical #2		Paid In Full !!!			5
Credit Card #1		Paid In Full !!!			12
Credit Card #2	$ 2,675	$ 50	$ 275	9.99%	
Credit Card #3	$ 5,875	$ 100	$ 100	19.99%	
LOC	$ 8,450	$ 100	$ 100	4.75%	
Car	$ 14,650	$ 265	$ 265	3.00%	
Mortgage	$ 44,925	$ 400	$ 400	4.50%	

Months #13 thru #24 - On to your next card. You should start to see a pattern. Now we can take the $225 a month we used to pay on the last card and *add it, ALL OF IT, to the $50 minimum monthly payment of the $3,000 card*. It will take you a couple of months into Year 3 to pay off this credit card in full with a $275 a month payment.

NOTE: We have rounded up the debts as we move further along to keep it a bit easier visually. Also, remember to continue to make minimum payments on your other debt trees, on time, every time, right? When you do, those other debts continue to diminish, albeit slowly.

After Year Two.

Table 7

Your Debt	Amount	Minimum Payment	Actual Payment	Interest Rate	Months to Pay Off
Credit Card #2		Paid In Full !!!			23
Credit Card #3	$ 5,875	$ 100	$ 100	19.99%	
LOC	$ 8,450	$ 100	$ 100	4.75%	
Car	$ 14,650	$ 265	$ 265	3.00%	
Mortgage	$ 44,925	$ 400	$ 400	4.50%	

Months - #25 thru #60. By now, I know you understand the next step of your payment plan. You take the $275 a month you no longer pay on Credit Card #2 and apply all of it to the $100 a month payment of Credit Card #3. Credit Card #3 has about a $5,875 balance so it will take you less than 2 years to pay off your last credit card at $375 a month.

I want you to understand what I just said. Say this out loud. "I paid off two medical bills, a tax lien and ALL of my credit card debt in just 41 months."

How would that feel? Can you imagine it? Can you dream it? Then you can do it, but it gets even more fun in a moment.

At the End of Year 4.

Table 8

Your Debt	Amount	Minimum Payment	Actual Payment	Interest Rate	Months to Pay Off
Credit Card #3	Paid In Full !!!				41
LOC	$ 7,270	$ 100	$ 100	4.75%	
Car	$ 9,000	$ 265	$ 265	3.00%	
Mortgage	$ 39,575	$ 400	$ 400	4.50%	

At the End of Year 5.

You know the drill. You now have $325 a month to tack on to your line of credit payment of $100. This means it will take you about two years, **or a total of 58 months,** at the new payment of $425.00 a month, every month, to pay off your Line of Credit.

Table 9

Your Debt	Amount	Minimum Payment	Actual Payment	Interest Rate	Months to Pay Off
LOC	Paid In Full !!!				58
Car	$ 5,200	$ 265	$ 265	3.00%	
Mortgage	$ 36,725	$ 400	$ 400	4.50%	

Now remember you've made the minimum payments on your car for the entire time. Guess what. At month 68 *you will pay off your car as agreed.*

At the End of Year 6

Table 10

Your Debt	Amount	Minimum Payment	Actual Payment	Interest Rate	Months to Pay Off
Car	Paid In Full !!!				68
Mortgage	$ 30,825	$ 400	$ 400	4.50%	

If you do that, you will pay off your house in 35 more months. Do you understand what I'm telling you? Right now, you stand less than 10 years away from having no debt - without having to get another job, hock a wedding ring, or sell a pint of blood and you slashed 5 years off your house mortgage to boot.

At the End of Year 7

Table 11

Your Debt	Amount	Minimum Payment	Actual Payment	Interest Rate	Months to Pay Off
Mortgage	$ 19,100	$ 400	$ 400	4.50%	

How does the balance look now?

At the end of Year 8 ...

Table 12

Your Debt	Amount	Minimum Payment	Actual Payment	Interest Rate	Months to Pay Off
Mortgage	$ 6,850	$ 400	$ 400	4.50%	

Before the end of Year 9.

Table 13

Your Debt	Amount	Minimum Payment	Actual Payment	Interest Rate	Month Paid Off
Mortgage		Paid in Full !!!			103

*Mortgage **PAID IN FULL...***

**Now close your eyes,
really close your eyes,
and imagine...**

YOU CUT DOWN YOUR ENTIRE DEBT FOREST!

The "Hope is Not a Plan" PLAN compared to Pyramiding Your Payments

Let's start with the Tax Lien and two collections, under the Hope is Not a Plan method. We have no idea when, if ever, they would have been paid.

I'll cut you some slack and say you would have paid the tax lien within two years because your local government would have proceeded with a tax foreclosure leaving you sleeping in a cardboard box if you hadn't paid it. As for the collections, go past "go" and head towards never - never land.

Table 14

Hope is NOT a Plan Plan

Your Debt	Amount	Minimum Payment	Interest Rate	Months to Pay Off	Approx. Interest Paid in $
Credit Card #3	$ 6,000	$ 100	19.99%	247	18708
Credit Card #2	$ 3,000	$ 50	9.99%	48	626
LOC	$ 10,000	$ 50	4.75%	127	2690
Mortgage	$ 50,000	$ 400	4.50%	168	17244
Car	$ 20,000	$ 265	3.00%	84	2130
Credit Card #1	$ 1,000	$ 25	2.99%	20	24
Med Col #2	$ 1,000	$ -	Late Fee	?	?
Tax Lien	$ 400	$ -	Varies	?	?
Med Col #1	$ 400	$ -	Late Fee	?	?
Total	$ 91,800	$ 890	7.54	247	$ 41,422.00

I know, no one would ever take 247 months to pay off a credit card. How could it take that long if you pay the minimums? The next time you get a credit card statement, look for the box that credit card companies must legally include regarding payment schedules.

As with most things financial, I recommend you sit down, if you only make minimum payments on your debts. You may feel faint at how long you'll make those payments. If this sounds like you, bankers LOVE you...you pay our paychecks and bonuses.

Let me tell you the true story of a business owner who came to me during my first year in banking. She complained that she just wasn't making any headway on her line of credit debt with our bank. I pulled her payment history and she had made every single payment for 7 years...every single MINIMUM payment, on time, every time, all the time.

Either no one told her, she forgot or didn't understand, that she owned an "Interest Only Line of Credit." This type of loan only required a minimum payment for the amount of interest she accrued for the previous month.

Bottom Line, she still owed the entire $25,000 of principle she had borrowed (of course she maxed it out) after 7 years of minimum payments. Needless to say, she took out her emotional displeasure on me for the first 30 or so minutes.

Once she calmed down, I made her a promise - I told her I'd teach her another way to pay down her debt.

That day, I taught her the same Lumberjack plan I've described above. Of course, she also had maxed her credit cards, had a home mortgage, car payments etc. It took her 10 years to get debt free using the Lumberjack Debt Reduction plan. The last I looked, she had saved $19,000, paid cash for a car and helped her daughter with her college tuition.

Check out the difference between the two plans.

Table 15

Hope is NOT a Plan Plan

Your Debt	Amount	Minimum Payment	Interest Rate	Months to Pay Off	Approx. Interest Paid in $
Credit Card #3	$ 6,000	$ 100	19.99%	247	18708
Credit Card #2	$ 3,000	$ 50	9.99%	48	626
LOC	$ 10,000	$ 50	4.75%	127	2690
Mortgage	$ 50,000	$ 400	4.50%	168	17244
Car	$ 20,000	$ 265	3.00%	84	2130
Credit Card #1	$ 1,000	$ 25	2.99%	20	24
Med Col #2	$ 1,000	$ -	Late Fee	?	?
Tax Lien	$ 400	$ -	Varies	?	?
Med Col #1	$ 400	$ -	Late Fee	?	?
Total	$ 91,800	$ 890	7.54	247	$ 41,422.00

Table 16

Lumberjack Chopping Down Trees Plan

Your Debt	Amount	Minimum Payment	Interest Rate	Months to Pay Off	Approx. Interest Paid in $
Medical #1	$ 200	?	Late Fee	1	?
Tax Lien	$ 400	?	Varies	3	?
Medical #2	$ 1,000	?	Late Fee	5	?
Credit Card #1	$ 1,000	$ 25	2.99%	12	24
Credit Card #2	$ 3,000	$ 50	9.99%	23	345
Credit Card #3	$ 6,000	$ 100	19.99%	41	4231
LOC	$ 10,000	$ 100	4.75%	61	1725
Car	$ 20,000	$ 265	3.00%	68	2002
Mortgage	$ 50,000	$ 400	4.50%	104	13589

Please don't move on until you understand the difference between the two charts above. The first chart reflects the Hope is Not a Plan method of debt reduction - what most people do. If you fall in this group, don't feel bad. Neither our schools nor our parents ever taught us this.

The second chart reflects our Chopping Down Debt Trees plan. Under this philosophy, you actually lay out your debt and chop it down one by one with the simple process I outlined for you.

Do you want to pay, under our "usual way" example, over $40,000 in interest on your debt and take 20 years to pay everything off? Or, would you rather take 10 years less to find yourself personally debt free?

Not enough incentive? Believe it or not, I've had people not want to do this because they make their payments as agreed and don't want to change anything.

Guess they didn't trust evil bankers.

Table 17

Lumberjack Chopping Down Trees Plan

Your Debt	Amount	Minimum Payment	Interest Rate	Months to Pay Off	Approx. Interest Paid in $
Medical #1	$ 200	?	Late Fee	1	?
Tax Lien	$ 400	?	Varies	3	?
Medical #2	$ 1,000	?	Late Fee	5	?
Credit Card #1	$ 1,000	$ 25	2.99%	12	24
Credit Card #2	$ 3,000	$ 50	9.99%	23	345
Credit Card #3	$ 6,000	$ 100	19.99%	41	4231
LOC	$ 10,000	$ 100	4.75%	61	1725
Car	$ 20,000	$ 265	3.00%	68	2002
Mortgage	$ 50,000	$ 400	4.50%	104	13589
Total	$ 91,600	$ 940	7.54	104	$ 21,916.00
YOUR Savings				143	$ 19,506.00

Imagine, after month 104 you actually put away over $13,500 in savings over the next 12 months. Remember, after month 104, you no longer have $1,140 a month in debt payments. In two years, you could pay cash for your car. Not to mention, you saved over $19,000 in Interest you WOULD have paid to the banks.

> *Your choice. Which Plan would you choose?*
> An Evil Banker's vote - Hope is Not a Plan.
> I Vote the Lumberjack Chopping Down Trees Plan.
> **The only VOTE that counts? YOURS.**

 ## You have to TACKLE this BOX

____ Obtain your Credit Report and go through it with a fine toothed comb.

____ If you have a government tax lien and/or judgment, take every extra dollar and pay these off first. Government SCARES everyone, but especially banks. Take anything you pay extra on any other debt and apply it to these first. Keep making minimum payments on everything else.

____ Rank your CHARGE OFFS from smallest to largest, after you pay the government, and repay your charge offs. Require they send you documentation of your complete payoffs and make sure the Credit Bureaus reflect it on your report.

____ If you dispute a charge off - document all of your discussions and work with the vendor and credit bureaus to get it resolved and removed from your credit report.

____ Make your Debt Pyramid. Put the smallest at the top and the next smallest and so on. Put this on paper or in a spreadsheet with your Balance, your Minimum Payment, and your Interest Rate.

____ **Lumberjacking** -Take EVERY extra dollar you have (including extra payments you may be making somewhere else) and put it on the smallest until you completely **CHOP** down this debt.

____ Now take the payment from your paid off debt and apply it **totally** to the minimum payment of your next smallest debt. Continue to pay extra on this debt until paid and so on until you chop it all down.

____ Start saving your former payments so that you can become your own bank. Then, in the future, borrow from yourself and pay yourself back when you need a loan.

Chapter 4

Applying for a Loan

How can you position yourself to get an approved loan?

One more time - do you really NEED this loan?

Seriously, before you proceed, even though you bought this book to learn Super - Secret Financial Tips to change your life and your children's lives, before you borrow or if you're already in debt, can you earn more money, cut expenses, sell off equipment you don't use, anything to avoid borrowing the money?

I'm begging you to try every other avenue to avoid borrowing. Again, how many bankers have ever asked or recommended this to you?

If you do, you'll save a ton of money. A $10,000 loan for 5 years 4% costs you a monthly payment of $184.17 a month - **EVERY MONTH for 5 Years** - and a total of $1,049.92 in compounded interest.

So, you paid the bank over $1000 to borrow $10,000 when you could have paid the money back to yourself over the same 5 - year period. You would have $11,049.92 in the bank if you "managed" your money, and would save $10,000 you can "lend" back to yourself.

Now imagine $10,000 on a credit card at 9.99% (or worse). and now you're paying $212.42 a month (every month) and a total of $2745.30 in total interest over five years - if you pay $212.42 and not the $25 or $50 minimum payment.

Would you like to get even sicker to your stomach? How many extra hours do you have to work to earn $1,000 or nearly $3,000?

Ok, for the last time, I'm going to encourage you to save, cut expenses, work more hours, sell equipment you don't use - anything - before you apply for a loan.

Alright, I'm stepping off my soapbox now.

You always want to be *prepared to borrow* long before you actually *need to borrow*. Remember, a loan process may take a couple days, maybe a week, or a month or a year. The amount of time it takes depends on your preparation and the size, complexity and type of the loan request.

The stronger you are from a debt standpoint, the better your credit score, the more collateral (your home, cars, other assets) you have to offer, and the amount of liquidity (money you have in bank accounts), will all determine the time it takes to get an answer, to get the loan closed and to get your money. As an old football coach once said -

"Preparation Meets Opportunity"

In other words, **your** preparation can result in **your** positive lending opportunity. Everything **you** can gather, everything **you** can improve financially will decrease the time **you** will spend waiting for **your** loan approval. Further, **you'll** usually get better terms and lower interest rates. Note a trend here?

I can promise you that everything **you** make the time to prepare before you go into the bank/credit union will save you days/weeks/months compared with walking in unprepared to the lender.

If applying for the loan is the first question, then *who will guarantee your request* is the second. As an individual or a couple, you have to address the personal guarantor position of a loan.

I call this the left arm/first child question. Who's backing this request with a personal, unconditional guarantee of the loan? Remember, everything we've discussed about credit score, debt, net worth etc. above, applies to anyone listed as a guarantor.

In other words, if you boast an 800 - credit score and your partner has a 500 - credit score, there's a good chance you'll receive a decline letter in the mail. In fact, I'd recommend you have the credit score discussion early in your relationship and before you make it legal. Otherwise, you both may be in for some big financial surprises.

If you know, someday, you'll need to borrow money, here's few things to think about and try to improve.

Have you ever watched the comedian Jeff Foxworthy? He's a good old boy who loves the outdoors. Jeff has a routine that I'll paraphrase to help you understand how long it takes to get a loan applied for, reviewed, approved, documented and closed...even a great request can take weeks and a "hairy" one, months.

So, as with fishing, **be patient** - your loan officer doesn't get paid unless he/she closes the loan. In other words, I want the loan closed as fast as you do, so I can get on to my next loan and make more money. I'm not the enemy.

If you have a lower than 700 credit score - you might be delayed.

If your property or equipment appraisal comes in below 100% of the amount you're asking for - you might be delayed.

If you've maxed out your credit cards - you might be delayed.

If you've never taken out a loan - you might be delayed.

If you owe Uncle Sam, your state or city taxes you can afford to pay - you might be delayed.

If you don't have at least 10% and usually 20% to put down on a loan - you might be delayed.

If you have plead guilty or been convicted of a non-violent and non-financially related felony - you might be delayed.

If you're late on one or two payments on your credit cards, car, house or any business reporting to the credit bureau - you might be delayed.

> If you don't have a legal survey to your property - you might be delayed.
>
> **If you're a participant in any legal action - you might be delayed.**
>
> If your "property" sits on a property owned by a relative who promises to will it to you when they die - you might be delayed.
>
> **If your neighbor is a gas station, dry cleaner, nuclear power plant, radioactive material manufacturer - you might be delayed.**
>
> If you're weak in 1 or at most 2 of the following: guarantor credit, personal net worth, personal liquidity, collateral, or environmental concerns or if you own a business - you might be delayed.

Do you see a pattern here? Who caused all of these delays? **YOU.** If you don't ensure these are all non-issues, you will delay your loan request and possibly cause its decline and your banker can't do a thing about it.

Patience - Feel free to call or email weekly to check in on progress; but DAILY calls/emails just take your banker away from your and other's requests.

If you seek a loan to refinance real estate you currently own, you may want to sit down when you get the valuation on your collateral. The Great Recession dropped property values in some places 30 - 50% from previous highs. I've actually had property owners weep tears in my office when I told them the current value of their property.

The good news? Real estate is recovering, but expect banks and credit unions to only use *at best* 80% Loan to Value (Example: lender will lend $80,000 for every $100,000 worth of value) and in some cases even less.

Let's talk about the importance of collateral - like your home, your business and all your assets. When you pledge your large assets to the bank as collateral, your financial institution will do everything legally within their power to make sure you pay back your loan so you don't lose your **ASS**ets (home, cars, etc.).

Banks/credit unions never want to make it easy to back out of a loan. In fact, as a lender, we want you to feel unbearable pain at the thought of not paying your debt as agreed.

As long as you always pay on time, every time and at least the minimum amount required on your loan, you never have to worry about losing your home, property or any other loan collateral. If you want collateral to become an issue, just stop paying as agreed on your loan.

Speaking of which, if you've had a history of issues with your finances, you may want to review the following to save you and all the lenders in your area time, money and effort.

Earlier we talked about comedian Jeff Foxworthy and how you can delay your loan. Now let's use his good buddy Bill Engvall's routine to talk about application declines.

If you have a lower than 600 credit score - here's your DECLINE.

If your property or equipment appraisal comes in below 50% of the amount you're asking for - here's your DECLINE.

If your credit cards are all maxed so you quit paying on them months ago - here's your DECLINE.

If you've declared bankruptcy in the last 5-7 years - here's your DECLINE.

If your credit report has more "charge offs" than "current paids," here's your DECLINE.

If you failed to disclose the dripping barrels of goo, the state mandated clean up, the glowing stuff on the back of your property - here's your DECLINE

If you owe Uncle Sam, your state or city taxes and you don't have a dime to pay them - here's your DECLINE.

If you take cash sales from your business and put them in your left pocket - leaving you no money to pay your bills according to your tax returns - here's your DECLINE.

If you don't have a dime to put down on the loan - here's your DECLINE.

If you're late on every one of the payments on your credit cards, car, house or any business reporting to the credit bureau - here's your DECLINE.

If you won't pay for a legal survey to your property - and you can't prove what you own - here's your decline.

If you have three or more "delay" issues as described earlier - here's your DECLINE.

If you have plead guilty or been convicted of a violent and/or financially related felony - here's your DECLINE.

If your "property" sits on a property owned by a relative who promises to will it to you when they die - but won't transfer the title or guarantee your loan request - here's your DECLINE.

If you're weak in 3 or more of the following: business cash flow, guarantor credit, personal net worth, business and personal liquidity, collateral, or environmental concerns - here's your DECLINE.

Again, see a pattern - **YOU**. If you have any or all (gulp) of the issues described above - make sure you have LOW expectations regarding qualifying for a loan.

Oh, you can invest hours of your time gathering all the financial information hoping to find that one "DORK FISH" (Bill Engvall description of the dumbest fish in the lake) banker blinded by your personality to ignore your financial challenges and approve your request, ah, NOPE won't happen.

> REALITY CHECK - you're fishing in a lake deprived of oxygen with NO HOPE of landing a fish (loan). Save your time and your banker's time - start resolving the issues we've described.

Yes, it may take years. Yes, your financial situation may not survive the wait. Yes, you'll spend hours cleaning up the Lake Erie mess YOU created. However, I guarantee it won't clean itself, so get to it. Until then...

Here's your DECLINE.

I can't tell you how many people I've talked to, often married couples, who decided not to pursue their dream loan request after I cover collateral and personal guarantees.

"I want to make sure you totally understand what you've pledged as collateral and unconditional personal guarantees. If you fail to meet your monthly payments, we will foreclose on this agreement.

> **Please note:** I'm not telling you NEVER to borrow. I'm trying to convey the reality of borrowing money. Unfortunately, too many folks learn this much too late.

We will sell all your personal assets until the bank/credit union receives payment in full. Do you both understand completely what you have offered in the way of personal guarantees and collateral?"

Let's just say those questions sometimes change the poker faces of the applicants. Now they understand the difference between *wanting something and needing something.*
In all honesty, bankers don't want anyone to know a dirty little secret - we hate collateral. We really don't want it and we don't want to have to sell it. We want you to pay the bank back with interest – which makes the bank money.

Banks usually lose money on foreclosures. Having to go through the legal process to liquidate collateral costs hours of time, stacks of paperwork and thousands of dollars. In other words, we lose money on foreclosures. We don't want your collateral, your home, your cars, your assets, but we'll take them if you quit paying as agreed.

As the applicant, you want to walk into your bank or credit union understanding that you will need to offer your personal guarantee and some form of collateral for most loan requests. Further, you must pay your loan in full or face consequences that will change your life forever.

Bonus question to ask and impress your banker at your first meeting.

"Can you please tell me the total interest I'll pay the bank/ credit union"

(say if I take out 3,4,5 - year loan for a car or 10, 15, 20, or 30 - year home loan).

You need to know how much this loan REALLY costs you.

Understand, as a banker, we know, more times than not, the person (people) asking for a loan doesn't know what questions they should ask.

Ask and impress your banker with some more bonus questions at your first meeting.

"Can you explain ALL the closing costs associated with your loan?"

"May we negotiate your bank commitment fee?" You pay a bank commitment fee above and beyond your interest paid and you may negotiate it.

"What appraisal options do you offer?" You will usually pay less for a drive-by appraisal as opposed to a full appraisal.

"Please explain the pre - payment penalty?" If you agree to a pre-payment penalty, should you decide to pay of your loan early, you may have to pay this fee. Make sure you understand this (no I'm not kidding).

"When can I expect this loan to close?" Remember this can vary depending on complications.

"Do I get a copy of my appraisal?"

"Do I get a copy of my credit report?"

 ## You have to TACKLE this BOX

____ Gather every loan statement & credit card statement and list out the balances, minimum payments, and interest rates you pay.

____ Shop your loans & credit cards for better rates, terms and/or conditions.

____ Beware of the transfer fees, prepayment penalties, and the terms and conditions of the new loan or credit card.

____ Do the math and compare the savings. Unsure about the math, ask your banker to do it. Don't be embarrassed; when my car is broke, I take it to a mechanic. If you have broken finances, find a good accountant or banker to help you repair them.

____ If you HAVE to take out a loan, understand what you need to give the banker and position yourself for an approval with the best rates and terms.

TACKLE THIS NOW.

Chapter 5

Co-signing a Loan: Becoming an Additional Guarantor

Again, I want you to look each other in the eye (no partner - then look in the mirror) and ask

"Will they ever stop paying on this loan? If not, then what?"

In the beginning of this book, we talked about you wanting to borrow money. Now let's discuss when a loved one or friend "wants" or even "needs" to borrow money and can't. For any number of reasons, a bank/credit union declined their request to borrow; but,

---

And this is a

BIG BUT,

---

the bank told your family member/friend *IF* they could just find a solid co-signer, their lender would reconsider the loan request.

So now, out of nowhere, this long lost relative/friend comes trudging over to your house. After a bunch of small talk, how you doing, boy this is some weather, **ummm** I need to get a loan for a car/house/student loan, and the bank says I need a co-signer.

There you have it. You knew it was coming.

They go on to tell you how badly they NEED this loan, without it, they'll have to walk to work, sleep in a cardboard box or ask people if they want to supersize their drink or a hot apple pie for the rest of their lives. Then they drop the bomb.

"Would you please co-sign my loan?"

At this moment every emotion rips through your soul. Your son, your granddaughter, your nephew needs a helping hand. Maybe your parents co-signed your first car back in the day. What can it hurt?

It can hurt YOU a lot.

Let me tell you about the elderly mother and lazy-good-for-nothing son who came in, asking to start his business. Unfortunately, this was my first larger loan. I hadn't had enough experience to see what was coming and now I have to live with this forever.

In my years as a banker, I've come to learn that everyone has a dream. In this case, he dreamed of opening a doughnut shop. He came into my office with his mother. She used to own a restaurant and wanted to help him get started. She had penny pinched and saved with her late husband for years while owning their little restaurant. She had paid off her house on Lake Huron and had adequate savings plus $100,000 in a CD.

I had previously reviewed his application and declined it because **he** didn't have adequate cash flow and had credit issues. Now, he returns with his Mom. He wanted to see if we'd approve it if she applied as a co-signer. I could have stopped it, I guess. I should have tried to stop it. Except, she had an 800 - credit score and money in the bank. She wanted to help her son, and by law, I had to take the application.

A very long and sad story later, he opened the doughnut shop. I never saw him there much, but I saw her there every hour of every day. Or so it seemed. Usually, I saw her there alone.

They used their remaining loan proceeds to make their payments for as long as that money held out. Then I got the call, the call all lenders HATE to get.

"Michael, we can't make this month's payment and we have to close." He didn't even have the guts to call me. Mom called me and I got sick to my stomach - literally.

We went through the entire foreclosure process. We liquidated Mom's $100,000 that took her a lifetime to save, foreclosed on her house that she had put up as additional collateral, her credit score plummeted and I never saw Mr. Good-for-Nothing again.

I see her in town all the time. She always smiles and still thanks me for helping her through the process. On occasion, she says she wishes things had turned out better. She has told me the one-bedroom apartment she lives in is "really nice" and all she can afford on her limited Social Security income.

She mentioned her son recently. "Michael, he's really trying hard, you know. I saw him last week. He needed a little money to get by. I know he's trying."

I have three rules of life that often come up in banking:

You Can't Stop Stupid
You Can't Cure Crazy
You Can't Teach Happy

On the surface, this story seems Stupid, qualifies as Crazy and seems Sad. When it comes to family, especially children or grandchildren, **remove all bets**. I've seen completely rational people do Stupid financial things that seemed unbelievably Crazy in an effort to make their family member Happy.

STOP...

Before you Co-Sign a loan document for anyone - STOP.

You need to completely understand your legal, binding pledge before you become a co-signer or additional guarantor on ANY loan document.

Bottom line? Who will own this loan? You. Yes, <u>YOU</u>.

As the lender, I want to make my client happy and I get paid if and when I make loans. If someone I've declined can mitigate the reasons for the decline, I legally have to accept the new application and consider it.

If they can find a (unsuspecting, rich, high credit score, no-debt sap) co-signer strong enough to change my decision, great for them. If the said co–signer's little old grandmother sincerely just wants to help her grandson, I CAN'T legally stop her. However, if the original borrower makes the payments a month or two late, it affects the co-signers credit score.

If the borrower, quits making the payments altogether, as the lender I **WILL** call the co-signer and **EXPECT THE CO-SIGNER** to start making the payments.

If the borrower AND the co-signer can't make the payments as agreed, the bank **WILL** report both to the credit bureau and **foreclose and liquidate all the collateral offered for the loan**.

So, before you "co-sign" ANY loan document, ask yourself if you potentially want to jeopardize your lake-front home, your lifetime of savings and your credit score, *so someone the bank already turned down for a loan can control your financial well-being until you pay their loan completely.*

Remember the Can't Stop Stupid Rule? Let me ask you this: How do banks make a lot of their profits? By making loans. So, as a banker, if I make money by making loans (that get paid back as agreed upon), you have to ask yourself as a co-signer, why did the bank decline this loan from the borrower? Why do they need a co-signer?

Then you have to ask yourself, if the bank declined the loan request is it STUPID for me to co-sign on this loan when the bank SHOUTED OUT TO THE WORLD "You're Declined" to the borrower?

In other words, who's STUPID if this loan goes bad? The borrower? No, they got the loan they wanted when they added you as a co-signer.

The bank? No, they've got the financial strength, collateral, and the credit score they needed to legally, ethically and within regulations, approve the borrowers request when they added YOU as a co-signer.

Let's see, the borrower got what he wanted, and the bank got what it wanted. But now Jr. isn't paying his loan as agreed which got the co-signer a call from the bank, a new loan payment and/or a foreclosure and financial headaches. Why?

Because the co-signer DIDN'T listen to the bank when they DENIED the borrower in the first place.

So, I ask you, who's Stupid in this scenario? Who seems, in hindsight, like they were Crazy and who isn't HAPPY now and for the foreseeable future? The CO-SIGNER. Think very seriously before you Co-sign any note. It could change your LIFE.

You must TACKLE this BOX

____ Once you have your financial life in order, you will have someone ask you to Co-sign a Loan, be prepared. What might you say?

____ If you Co-sign a loan, remember, it's your LOAN.

____ Understand if you Co-sign a loan, it may negatively impact your Cash Flow to a point that **you** are declined for a loan you want/need.

____ If a bank/credit union, who makes money making loans, declines someone, why should you "approve" them?

____ If you Co-sign a loan for someone and they QUIT paying, it will NEGATIVELY affect your credit score, just as if **you** quit paying a loan. Worse, you might not know it until it's already hit your credit report.

____ If you want to help someone, either save enough on your own to loan it to them or even take out the loan on your own and have them pay it back to you. I don't like this idea, but at least you have control of the payments to your bank/credit union.

____ Ask yourself, do you really want this (headache) responsibility if your life is quiet and happy?

____ If you give someone a loan from personal funds, put it in writing, no different than a bank/credit union and take a legal lien position on their collateral.

Chapter 6

Titles on Your Financial Accounts

> *The Next Time you open your statements, check how they're titled.*

The next time you get a statement in the mail for your checking account, savings account, safety deposit boxes, investments, insurances, titles of vehicles and deeds of properties, or any other assets, take an extra look and see how you "titled" your account.

At your bank or credit union, how you titled your account actually determines who can get information about your account, who can close it, who can deposit into it or withdraw from it. It can also determine who can add signers to the account or change it in any way.

Keep in mind, it doesn't matter who you meant to have on the account. It doesn't matter that you hired your lawyer to create your Trust. Maybe you just opened your statement, only to see that you still have your good-for-nothing ex-son-in-law on your account. UGH...

For example, sometimes older folks will come into a bank and want to put their children or a child on their accounts. I always present the option of making one of them their Power of Attorney (POA) instead of just adding them to their accounts as another option.

As a POA, the designee DOESN'T own the account. The POA can make deposits, withdraws, ask questions, receive information and in some cases open or close accounts. You can even designate your POA to buy real estate, borrow money, and make investments on your behalf. However, **as a POA, they hold absolutely no ownership in any of the assets**.

If, on the other hand, you put your child (or anyone else for that matter) on your account(s) as a full signer, they also own the account. This means they can still deposit, withdraw, or get information about the account and close the account.

However, as an owner, they don't have to make an accounting of their transactions. In fact, the funds in the account will be viewed by the bank and the courts as owned by **ALL** signers. Needless to say, this differs greatly from the rights and responsibilities of POA. Withdrawing funds from an account as a POA, as set out in a legal document, means they have authority over the account as the legal representative of the owner.

However, if you make them a *titled signer,* they legally own the money as much as you do!

If you should become incapacitated, the other signer on the account can continue to operate the account just as a POA. However, if you should die, the POA ceases whereas a legally titled signer can continue to withdraw the funds from this account as they see fit.

If you added an individual to your account and you pass away, *they own the account*. Period. Even if your Will says one thing, the remaining owner on the account can say another thing as it's still their account by right of ownership.

Another reason to consider a POA over an account signer is that as an owner of the account, your other signer's legal issues can affect your assets. If, for example, your other signer has a court order to seize their financial assets, *your joint account could be at risk*.

If you want your family to avoid a long, drawn out court battle, you may want to designate a POA instead of adding

the person as a signer. As always, seek the consultation of your attorney to help you decide.

In conclusion, I'm not recommending any particular titling of your checking and savings accounts. Nor am I suggesting you don't add someone as a signer/account owner or that you HAVE to add only POA's to your account. I am suggesting that YOU sit down with your children, your relatives and/or your attorney to determine what is best for YOU.

Review the titles on all your financial accounts. If you experience the death of a signer, or a change in health, remember only the remaining account owner can add a POA or a Trust as part of Estate Planning. Remember, **IF you don't bring in the documentation (like a POA or Trust) to your bank/credit union and request the title change, it hasn't officially happened.**

Again, PLEASE check your statement title.

Better yet, make an appointment with your financial institutions and *do an account review*. Go over your name, address, phone number, email address, signers, and other data currently on your accounts.

Ask your banker, financial advisor, and/or attorney to go through each of your accounts and confirm they're structured exactly the way you want them, with the signers you want, and the current account information is correct.

 ## You must TACKLE this BOX

____ Gather ALL your Bank Statements.
____ Gather ALL your Insurance Statements. (Life, Disability, Car, Home, etc.).
____ Get Your Safety Deposit Box Annual Bill.
____ Gather ALL your Investment Statements.
____ Grab the Title for ALL your cars.
____ Find the deed for your Home and ALL other Properties.
____ Review and Update the titling on the accounts. Make sure each is titled **exactly how you want**.
Make sure if these are not titled in a Trust that you've **added** beneficiaries or other signers to protect your assets.
____ If you are unsure of the titling, ask your professional banker, insurance agent, or financial advisor a couple of simple questions: What happens to this account if I die? What happens to this account if I'm incapacitated?
____ If you still have ANY doubts, consult your attorney for further direction.

TACKLE THIS NOW.

Chapter 7

Power of Attorney

> You're in an Accident.
> You're suffering from Dementia.
> You've Fallen Very Ill.
> **Who do you want to take care of you and your bills**

A *Power of Attorney (POA)* legally designates someone to act on another's behalf in most or all legal, financial, and even health matters. In fact, someday a POA may actually act *against* the wishes of the grantor (*now suffering from dementia*) of the power of attorney.

We've covered Power of Attorney (POA) in the last chapter as part of a Trust. I really can't think of a Trust where the owners of the Trust didn't also designate a Power of Attorney. However, consider this scenario where even within a Trust, a lady encountered a nightmare unforeseen when they established their Trust.

A married couple, fairly young and in good health established a trust. Who might they designate as a Trustee and Power of Attorney? Typically, each other or maybe parents. Now flash forward, ten, twenty, forty years. The married couple has aged, they've each started experiencing health problems and now have children and they haven't updated/looked at their Trust or Power of Attorney documents in a long time.

I had a client who had set up Trusts with her husband early in their marriage. They named each other as their Administrators. He suddenly and unexpectedly preceded her in death. When she came in to discuss her accounts, I asked her when she had last reviewed her Trust because she had titled her accounts in the name of the trust. She said she couldn't remember; her husband handled all those things.

I pulled her Trust document only to find it named her and her late husband as Trustees. Then I saw it named her son as Successor Trustee, except I knew he'd died a few months earlier (such is the life of a small-town banker).

Bottom line? She didn't have anyone alive who could serve as her Trustee because she no longer had a living Successor Trustee. Had anything happened to her, by death or incapacitation, her family would have faced months in court, even though she had a Trust, a Will and POA documents.

Revisit Your Trust/POA/Will

These LIVING legal documents, must change as your circumstances change. As time passes, you need to address **any LIFE** changes in **any** of these documents.

As mentioned above, having a POA in place can aid you in handling your affairs should you suffer incapacitation. However, please understand, if your POA opens an account in your name but doesn't place you on the account, a bank will only allow access, information, withdraws, and so forth **by the POA**.

On occasion, this can cause tensions to rise with the grantor of the POA. In some cases, when the courts appoint a POA to oversee a person's finances, it can bring its own can of worms into family relationships.

As with everything legal, consult your attorney for direction before granting POA to anyone. You can also retain your rights on a bank account and still add a POA to the account. Make sure you completely understand the protections, responsibilities and expectations of your POA when you establish this person with your Attorney.

 ## You must TACKLE this BOX

____ Do you have a POA?
____ Do you need a POA?
____ If you're injured, incapacitated, suffer from dementia or other health issues, who will handle your finances?
____ If you're injured, incapacitated, suffer from dementia or other health issues, or die, who will handle your spouse's finances?
____ If you have a POA, is this person still able, healthy, & competent to handle these duties?
____ Have you or your spouse experienced any health issues? Are you at or nearing retirement age?
____ If you encounter life-threatening challenges, who will make your continued care decisions?

Look over your answers and make an appointment to consult an attorney or consider an online legal service to establish a POA. Make sure to do your research.

TACKLE THIS NOW.

Chapter 8

Beneficiaries, Payable on Death, In Trust For

You're Dead – Now What?

The Benefits of keeping the Court out of your Death

I've talked about your POA, a Will and a Trust. However, what if you don't have a Will or a Trust and can't afford to get one right now?

You need to head straight to all of your financial institutions and declare your *Account Beneficiaries* or *"In Trust For" Designees*, depending upon your state laws. In some states this can also be referred to as *"Payable on Death"* (POD).

Although I realize paying for a Will or establishing a Trust has a cost, again a simple Will, **will** save your estate thousands of dollars and your children/relatives hours in the courtroom. I also know you can afford **ten minutes** out of one day to sit down with your banker to update your account information and title.

Please understand. If you die, your banker will pull up the information on EACH of your accounts to determine who can have access to your funds. The legal options for access to a bank account are any other person who is:

1) a legally titled owner;
2) the named beneficiary as "in trust for" (ITF); or payable on death (POD) designee depending upon the state in which you reside.
3) Designee/representative named by the Court.

Your banker should know which designation applies within your state. When you designate an account "In Trust For" (ITF), it ensures that the funds within this account will transfer to the ITF designee with little issue.

Typically, your bank will require a legal death certificate for the last living title holder on the account and a current and legal form of identification for the named beneficiary. Note, a couple of very important requirements: First, for the bank to allow transfer of funds AND/OR any information on the account to a named ITF, ***all titled owners must have passed away and death certificates filed and presented to the bank.***

In other words, if there are two titled owners on the account, like a husband and wife, and the husband preceded the wife in death two years earlier and then she dies but (AND THIS DOES HAPPEN) no one brought in the husband's death certificate to have him taken off the account, the beneficiary would have to produce **BOTH DEATH CERTIFICATES** to the bank.

Second, keep in mind that if any owner remains alive, they can make any changes they want, at any time, to the titling of the account, the beneficiary designation or ITF/POD. (POD is similar to the ITF in that it pays the balance of the account to one or more beneficiaries upon the passing of the primary account holder).

Understand, the bank isn't a court of law. So, if the account doesn't have an ITF/POD, as a survivor, the bank will NOT tell anyone a thing unless ordered by a court. If the beneficiary can't produce a death certificate, the bank will NOT distribute funds or release information on the account - even to the named beneficiary.

In fact, the bank/credit union shouldn't even confirm nor deny that a person is, in fact, a beneficiary on an account without a proper death certificate or a court order. So, if you're a grandchild waiting on a grandparent, who is loaded, to kick the proverbial bucket, you CAN'T go into the bank to see if you're getting any proceeds from their accounts.

I've had people get downright ticked because they were named as a POD/ITF on an account, they even had a statement, but without the title holder of the accounts present, a legal death certificate, or direction from a judge, the bank **is prohibited by law** to release any information on the accounts.

I recommend that you (and your spouse) gather every one of your bank, credit union, investment, insurance, and financial statements first. Then, just look at the title on the accounts. If you see one name and nothing else, start praying for that person's continued good health.

If you see two names, that's better. If you see one or two names followed by ITF or POD and a name, you have an account with one legal signer or more and a named beneficiary in the event of the passing of the last legal owner of the account.

If you are incapacitated, the bank will ONLY allow access to your account by another person on the title who provides legal identification as proof of their identity. Earlier I mentioned that the bank/credit union is not a court of law. Understand if there's a legal beneficiary named as ITF/POD who produces a legal death certificate and identification, the bank/credit union should/will allow that person to withdraw the funds by way of a bank check.

WAIT... We have a will and the will says....

It doesn't matter to the bank what the Will says. We're bankers not the judges. We will issue funds upon death if a named ITF/POD produces a death certificate and identification. Period. Now, you or others may legally contest that in a court of law (and often do). However, the bank has served its role as a secure financial institution.

Let me tell you about the little eighty-something lady, who had seven different accounts with her husband and she was a co-signer on every one of them.

Her husband, however, had eight accounts (the seven with her), including the one with their life savings of $65,000. Unfortunately, on this account, he hadn't added her as a signer or as a beneficiary.

What did that mean for her? She spent eight months in and out of probate court. She spent over $3000 in attorney and court fees to have a judge award her the funds in his account.

It would have taken less than five minutes, his driver's license and his signature **while he was alive** to avoid that misery. Unfortunately, his Will didn't change how we had to handle this situation at the bank and it broke my heart. As a result, I don't want that to happen to you or anyone else.

Adding a POD/ITF beneficiary takes about 10 minutes.

You usually need to have their legal name, social security number, address, phone number and sometimes, an email address.

In most cases, a POD/ITF doesn't sign the signature card and usually doesn't have to be present to be added as a beneficiary. However, as with most financial matters, contact your financial institution to confirm their policies.

As a banker, I've basically covered bank scenarios; however, the same usually applies for investment accounts and insurance accounts. Make the time to contact your professionals in those fields and ask them what happens should you pass on and what do your heirs need to do and produce to access these accounts.

IF you love your kids, you'll take a few hours to ensure you've structured your financial assets/accounts exactly the way you want. I recommend that you sit down with them and lay out your intentions. Some people will write out instructions in addition to their Will/Trust to help the process.

In fact, I've known people who used the Masking Tape Method of asset distribution in addition to their Will or Trust. They literally took masking tape inscribed with the name of who would get an object when they died and placed it on the furniture and other valuables.

Now the masking tape method may not hold up in court, but it has to be better than the gross carnage of families literally grabbing, scratching and clawing for every little thing in dead Grandma's house.

So, if you want to legally ensure a specific person does (or does not) get a specific asset, then include it in your will or trust documents. Anything you can do to make sure future Christmas and Thanksgiving gatherings stay happy for your family is a great idea.

The more you can convey legally, like officially naming ITF/POD beneficiaries or creating a Will/Trust will help. Maybe even getting it down on a bit of tape and a marker will help let your survivors know your wishes.

Trust me, this is all far easier to do when you are alive. It's even easier to do when you're well. Take it from someone who's rushed documents to hospital beds and senior citizen homes, trying to finalize wishes and take care of everyone. It's not what you or your kids want to do in your last hours.

 ## You must TACKLE this BOX

____ Strongly consider drafting a legal Will or Trust.

____ In the last chapter, you gathered all of your statements. Make sure every financial account has a named Beneficiary linked to it.

____ Ask your Banker if you need to add a Payable on Death (POD) or an In Trust For (ITF) designation to your accounts and/or Safety Deposit Box.

____ Ask your Insurance Agent if you need to add a Beneficiary to your Insurance Policies.

____ Ask Your Financial Advisor if you need to add a Beneficiary to your investments.

____ Check your work benefit accounts, like pensions, insurance, spousal Insurance, 401k, etc. to be sure you have beneficiaries on each of the accounts.

____ *Review* your Payable on Death (POD) or a In Trust For (ITF) Beneficiary designations on your accounts and/or Safety Deposit Box to make sure they are still who you want as beneficiaries.

____ *Review*, with your insurance agent, the Beneficiary designations on your insurance accounts to verify they are still who you want as beneficiaries.

____ *Review* with your Financial Advisor the Beneficiary designations on your Investments accounts to make sure they are still who you want as beneficiaries.

Chapter 9

Last Will & Testament

Do you know what a Will is?
Do you have one?

If not, **the Court System**
WILL
decide what happens to
your money, your stuff and
your minor children
SHOULD YOU DIE unexpectedly.

Let's find out right now if you love your children. No children? Then do you like or love your nearest relative? Of course, you do, you say. How could I ask you such a ridiculous question?

Let's find out.

Do you plan to die? You think I'm kidding but in fact, I've never been more serious. DO YOU PLAN TO DIE someday? So far, the only thing I can guarantee is that if you bought this book, if you're reading this book, someday, you will die. We all do.

Do you have a written, signed, notarized Last Will & Testament? If the answer's yes, so far you like or love your children, spouse, or nearest relatives.

If the answer is no, then the harsh reality is, you must **NOT.** Why? Because how can you claim to like, love, or care about your next-of-kin if you haven't invested a few dollars (compared to not having one) and a couple hours of time into your Will?

Usually this is the most important legal document you'll ever have drawn up. To begin, you need to determine whether you require a *will-based estate plan* or a *trust-based estate plan*.

In the next chapter, I'll cover the trust-based estate planning, but before I do, remember **I'm NOT an attorney.** I'm not giving you **ANY** legal advice. I'm just a small-town country banker trying to help you avoid big time problems, for your heirs, after your death.

For our general purposes, your Will lays out your intentions about who will inherit your property, money and assets. It will also designate who you have selected to settle your final affairs.

When you select the most trusted person in your life as your *Personal Representative/Executor*, you're asking that person to settle all of your final financial obligations and distributions to your beneficiaries as laid out in your Will.

Sometimes, I say you must not "like" this most trusted person, because you're assigning them hours of responsibilities, phone calls, visits to banks, credit unions, government offices and attorneys. Whenever an Executor comes into my office to deal with deceased accounts, I always ask them what they did to deserve such an "honor." The smiles are rueful - when they can smile.

That being said, choosing the right, responsible person to serve in this capacity can either help ease the transition of your estate to your heirs or ignite a battle. In other words, choose this person wisely because they'll be dealing with money, property, assets and the friends, family and other designees named in your Will.

If you work with an Attorney to create your Will, he/she will assist you in establishing the powers you're assigning to your Personal Representative/Executor. As part of the process, YOU will also determine who will inherit your property, assets and money.

In addition, you'll also get to decide when and how your estate will be transferred to your heirs. If you have minor children, YOU will get to determine who will serve as legal Guardian of your minor children until they reach adulthood in most states.

If you retain the services of an attorney, creating a Will tends to cost you more money than using one of the many online legal document sources. Although working with an on-line form is better than nothing, you MUST do your own due-diligence to determine what suits you best. This means you have to make sure YOU understand the state and national laws governing your estate.

One of the most often asked questions I get from clients is whether they should have a *Will or a Trust*. Again, this is a legal question and you should ALWAYS consult your attorney about what's best for you.

Having said that, I consulted mine and here are a couple GENERAL thoughts regarding a Will versus a Trust.

If you have an estate less than $250,000 in total you may want to consider a Will.

If you have one property (your home) or no properties in your estate, a Will may suffice.

If you have less than $25,000 in cash, a Will may best for you.

If you have only one or two heirs to whom you plan to designate your assets, you might find a Will satisfactory.

Again, consult your Attorney and do your homework.

You need to know *what a Will DOESN'T do for you and your estate.*

A Will doesn't allow your Executor/Personal Representative to walk into the bank/credit union to withdraw funds from your account if you have passed away or if you're incapacitated and unable to handle your banking.

The <u>only</u> ways a Personal Representative/Executor can withdraw your funds are:

    1) if you named/titled them as a signer on your account;
    2) if you presented the bank/credit union with legal documents declaring your Personal Representative and/or Executor as your legal Power of Attorney;
    3) by a legal Court Order.

I can't tell you how many times I've had Executors and/or loved ones come into my bank needing to withdraw money from an account only to leave empty-handed and usually very upset. As a banker, I can only release funds as described above - **_Period._**

Remember the little older lady in her eighties, who had 7 different accounts with her husband and she was a co-signer on every one of them? **REMEMBER** her husband had **8 accounts**, including the one with their life savings of $65,000 - the same account _he didn't_ add her to as a signer or as a beneficiary? Remember how she spent 8 months in and out of probate court and over $3,000 in attorney and court fees to FINALLY get her money?

In Chapter 5, we covered Power of Attorney as it relates to your bank accounts. Understand, one of the major issues surrounding a Will is you usually HAVE TO BE DEAD, for someone to invoke the instructions of a Will.

A Trust coupled with Power of Attorney designations can direct how you want your affairs handled in death, or while living incapacitated. Again, you want to spend a couple hundred bucks to consult an attorney. Otherwise, your heirs will spend much, much more.

You must TACKLE this BOX

____ Do you LOVE your Children?
____ Do you HAVE a Will?
____ Have you reviewed your Will in the last year?
____ Have you selected an Executor?
____ Have you had any major Life Changes since you drafted your Will?
____ Has anyone died, who was in your will, since you drafted it? Including your spouse?
____ Has anyone had children who was in your will, since you drafted it? Including you.
____ Has anyone been divorced who was in your will since you drafted it? Including You.
____ If yes to any of the above, have you updated your Will to reflect these changes?

TACKLE THIS NOW.

Chapter 10

Trusts

Do you know what a Trust is and do you have one/need one?

If you don't have a Will or a Trust,

TRUST ME

the Court System will

decide what happens to your money, your stuff and your minor children **SHOULD YOU DIE** or become unable to handle your own affairs.

> **NOTE:** I've never had one of my clients create a trust without the assistance of an attorney. As a result, I can't recommend an online service for creating a trust.

As part of your Trust, you will still have a Last Will and Testament. You will want to ask your lawyer if you should name your Trust in your Last Will and Testament to handle any assets not otherwise listed within your Trust as further protection of your estate.

This may sound confusing, but a good lawyer will protect the assets not named/titled in your trust by way of making THE TRUST a benefactor of your Will. Again, I'm not a lawyer and am not offering legal advice other than to say you must consult your attorney regarding this topic.

Your trust will serve you in multiple capacities. First, you'll determine a person or people as your *Trust Administrator(s) or Trustee(s)*. You will also establish a *Successor Trustee* in the event your Trust Administrator(s)/Trustee(s) passes away or is/are no longer able to function in their Trust capacity.

As with the Will's Personal Representative/Executor, your Trustee/Administrator should be someone you trust completely and obviously "dislike" as much as we've already discussed, if not more. I say more because a Trust's Administrator/Trustee must administer the intent and assets of the Trust while *you are alive* **and** *as a result of your death*.

In other words, you may be assigning years and years of important responsibilities to this person for you, your financial landscape, and in some cases, your health and welfare, depending upon the instructions of the Trust.

Let's look at another scenario I hope never happens to you. I use this example with every client I meet. Let's take a married couple with young children. They decide to go on a long weekend romantic get-away. They drop their children off at grandma's house and head out.

On the highway, in a split second, they are run off the road. The husband dies immediately. His wife suffers major head trauma. They have a Will and all the family assets go to the surviving spouse - the wife/mom who is no longer capable of signing a check.

Unfortunately, they don't have a Trust or Power of Attorney in place on their checking accounts or to guide anyone regarding their bank accounts, financial assets and the guardianship of their children.

This means that someone will have to petition the court at a substantial cost to establish guardianship over a mom who is in a coma. They will have to also have to ask the Court for oversight of her financial assets, access to her checking and savings accounts and designate guardianship over the children. Understand, the Court ultimately decides these questions, regardless who petitions said Court.

Now, imagine this scenario in detail. Replace these folks with you and your spouse. Don't have a spouse or kids? Fine, you survive the accident, but don't have a trust or Power of Attorney. Your parent/relative/friend still need to go through the painful anguish of appearing before a judge to put that Power of Attorney in place.

What if you have multiple relatives who want to take control of you and your assets? Unfortunately, I've lost count of how many times this situation comes up, especially if you have a fair amount of money, assets or children. I've seen a number of loving families completely destroyed by these types of events. Again, you can avoid this scenario. Establish a Trust or designate a Power of Attorney to guide your bank, financial institutions and other legal entities about how you want your affairs handled. Without it in place, someone's heading to court and you may not like how it turns out.

Trusts and your Bank or Credit Union

Please don't make the mistake that many people do when they invest in the legal creation of a Living Trust and assume that your attorney called all of their banks, credit unions, financial institutions, investment advisors and alerted them to the Living Trust.

If _YOU_ don't direct your legal counsel to do this, and move to change the legal owner of your properties, investments, and bank/credit union accounts into the name of the trust, *these assets are still in their original title.*

What that means is, as the bank, if we are not presented the written trust and instructed to move the bank accounts into the name of the trust, we will not recognize the Trust or its instructions or Administrator unless directed to do so by a judge. **YOU** have to bring it into the bank/credit union and make the changes to your accounts.

Ouch. Money and Time wasted.

Again, I stress you must consult with your attorney what you want moved into the Trust and how you want it handled within the Trust. If you have assets you don't want in your new Trust, make sure to at least make your lawyer aware of this decision because they may want to note this in some capacity.

More important, if you don't want to move certain assets into your Trust, you need to make sure you have titled them in such a way that enables the transfer of your assets should you pass away or become incapable of handling them. Otherwise, your heirs are back in court and you spent a couple thousand dollars setting up a trust that does you and them no good.

I've had people come into my bank inquiring about an account of a deceased relative. They found a savings passbook, but they couldn't find any statements and the account owner didn't keep a record of the amount in the account. As the banker, I cannot tell them ANYTHING about the account. I can't tell them if it's still open, who's on the account or what amount of money is in the account. In other words, if it's not titled in the Trust and it has $8.57 in the account AND it's the only account NOT in the Trust, the heirs would have to go back to Court to get access to the account. Imagine spending $2,000 -$3,000 to only find $8.57 in an account just because it wasn't titled properly to transfer the asset at death or upon incapacitation.

In addition, most Trusts will also include your assignment of a *Financial, Physical and Emotional Power of Attorney*. In other words, most lawyers will have you select a person/people as Power of Attorney to administer your finances as we've discussed.

You also may want to establish someone to handle your affairs if you become mentally incapable of doing so. Unfortunately, in banking, we see far too many people in this situation trying to continue to handle their own affairs and squandering their financial resources.

Most trusts will also designate a *Power of Attorney* to someone who can legally determine what health-related procedures should be used with you and when to discontinue such measures.

In my state, the legal capacity of the Power of Attorney ends at the moment of the person's death. I've literally had a Power of Attorney come into my bank to do a transaction on behalf of an elderly gentleman on a Monday. Then, the elder passed away on Wednesday.

The POA came in to do additional banking on his behalf on Thursday and we legally couldn't allow him to access the account, make a withdraw or tell him the client even had an account anymore because he was no longer the legal POA on the account. We couldn't tell him a thing until we received a court order. To say the least, the POA was frustrated, though very understanding in this particular case.

No Will?

No Trust?

I can't stress this enough: **if you don't make the time to establish a Last Will and Testament or a Trust before you die, then the courts/government will decide your estate.** You heard me. The government will determine who gets what, who (your children) and how much.

So, do you really want government determining your fate? Do you like or love your nearest relative, your children, your heirs? Then get a Will or a Trust.

You must TACKLE this BOX

____ Do you need a Trust? Have you asked your attorney?
____ Have you reviewed your Trust in the last year?
____ Do you still want the same people as your Trustees?
____ Have you had any major life changes since you drafted your Trust?
____ Has anyone died who was in your Trust since you drafted it? Including your spouse?
____ Are the Trustees and Successor Trustees still alive and able to fulfill their duties?
____ Has anyone had children who was in your Trust since you drafted it? Including you.
____ Has anyone divorced who was in your Trust since you drafted it? Including you.
____ Have you opened any new banking accounts or bought property or large assets since your drafted/reviewed your Trust? If so, did you title these in the name of the Trust? If you didn't they **AREN'T** covered by the Trust...

TACKLE THIS NOW.

Conclusion

Looking for a Gift for the Hard to Buy for Relative or Friend?

I sincerely hope you have found at least one nugget of helpful financial information within these pages. In my career, I've had countless people tell me they wish someone had talked to them about these topics' years ago.

In the big picture, I actually hope you were bored to death and didn't learn a thing from this book. If that's the case, you should be THRILLED. You're in the minority, I can assure you. You should feel GREAT about your financial position.

We don't teach this stuff in schools and most of us didn't learn it from our parents. Do you have a son or daughter or financially challenged friend? If so, do them a favor and buy them a copy.

They might not thank you, but then again…

If you purchased this book through Amazon, I would greatly appreciate it if you could take a moment and leave a review. Thank you.

Comments, Suggestions & Reviews

If you have any suggestions for future financial tips books or comments and suggested corrections, please send them to

universalbankingu@gmail.com

If you purchased one of our books online, we encourage you to please leave a review.

Appendix

Personal Account Review – Blank

Debt Pyramid – Blank

Emergency Contacts – Blank

Personal Account Comparison - Blank

These are also available on our Banking University Website at:

www.universalbankingu.com

Personal Account Review – Blank Worksheet

Universal Banking University - Personal Account Review Sheet					
Name				Date	
Account Relationships					
Checking Account(s)	1st Signer	2nd Signer	Benficiary (Yes/No)	Average Deposits	Interest Rate
Savings Account(s)	1st Signer	2nd Signer	Benficiary (Yes/No)	Average Deposits	Interest Rate
CD Account(s)	1st Signer	2nd Signer	Benficiary (Yes/No)	Average Deposits	Interest Rate
Credit Cards	1st Signer	Rewards	Minimum Payment	Balance	Interest Rate
Mortgage(s)	1st Signer	Maturity	Minimum Payment	Balance	Interest Rate
Loans & Credit Cards	1st Signer	Maturity	Minimum Payment	Balance	Interest Rate
Online Banking	Yes/No	Bill Pay	Benficiary (Yes/No)	Security Questions	Alerts
Investment/Retirement	Yes/No	Where	Benficiary (Yes/No)	Monthly Investment	Other
Safety Deposit Box	1st Signer	2nd Signer	Benficiary (Yes/No)	Paid in Full	Renewal Date

Business Owner (Y/N)		Do Not Call (Y/N)		Follow Up Appt	
Will (Y/N)		Trust (Y/N)		Life Insurance (Y/N)	
Health Insurance (Y/N)		Long Term Care (Y/N)		POA (Y/N)	

Notes

Download free at www.universalbankingu.com

Debt Pyramid – Blank Worksheet

	Universal Banking University - Debt Pyramid Sheet					
	Month/Year _____					
Debts	Lender	Amount $0.00	Minimum Payment $	Interest Rate %	Actual Payment $	Remaining Balance $
1						
2						
3						
4						
5						
6						
7						
8						
9						
10						
11						
12						
13						
14						
15						
	Total					
Notes						

Update this monthly and hang it where you can see it everyday.

Download free at www.universalbankingu.com

Emergency Contacts – Blank Worksheet 1 of 2

Universal Banking University - Emergency Confidential Information — Page 1/2

Name: _____ **Date:** _____

Professional Relationships

Professional Relationships	Representative	Company	Address	Phone Number	Email	Account Number
Primary Bank						
Secondary Bank						
Safe/Safety Dep Box						
Primary Doctor						
Eye Doctor						
Dentist						
Specialist						
Specialist						
Retirement						
Investment						
Investment						
Health Insurance						
Life Insurance						
Car Insurance						
Home Insurance						
CPA/Accountant						
Financial POA						
Health POA						
Pharmacy						
Mail Order Pharmacy						
Hospital						
Other						
Other						
Other						
Notes						

Download free at www.universalbankingu.com

Emergency Contacts – Blank Worksheet 2 of 2

Universal Banking University - Emergency Confidential Information

Name: _____ **Date:** _____ Page 2/2

Professional Relationships

Professional Relationships	Representative	Company	Address	Phone Number	Email	Account Number
Will						
Will - Executor						
Trust						
Trust - Trustee 1						
Trust - Trustee 2						
Trust - Successor TT						
Business Primary Bank						
Bes. Secondary Bank						
Business Legal Docs						
Business Legal Docs						
Busines Legal Docs						
Rental Properties						
Rental Properties						
Car Insurance						

Computer/Program	Computer	Computer Location	Login ID	Password	Security Question/Answer	
Password						
Password						
Password						
Safe Combination						
Safety Deposit Box Key						
Other _____						
Other _____						
Notes						

Download free at www.universalbankingu.com

Personal Account Comparison Blank

Universal Banking University - Personal Account Comparison Sheet

Name					Date			
Account Relationships									

Checking Account(s)	Current Bank/Credit Union	Current Balance	Interest Rate	Fees	Proposed Institution	Interest Rate	Proposed Fees	Net Difference
Savings Account(s)	Current Bank/Credit Union	Current Balance	Interest Rate	Fees	Proposed Institution	Interest Rate	Proposed Fees	Net Difference
CD Account(s)	Current Bank/Credit Union	Current Balance	Interest Rate	Fees	Proposed Institution	Interest Rate	Proposed Fees	Net Difference
Credit Cards	Current Bank/Credit Union	Current Balance	Interest Rate	Fees	Proposed Institution	Interest Rate	Proposed Fees	Net Difference
Loans	Current Bank/Credit Union	Current Balance	Interest Rate	Fees	Proposed Institution	Interest Rate	Proposed Fees	Net Difference
Mortgage								
Car								
Car								
Equity								
Student								
Other								
Other								
Investment	Current Financial Advisor	Current Balance	Interest Rate	Fees	Proposed Institution	Interest Rate	Proposed Fees	Net Difference
Insurance	Current Insurance Agency	Current Balance	Interest Rate	Fees	Proposed Insurance	Interest Rate	Proposed Fees	Net Difference
Life								
Health								
Car								
Dental								
Persciption								
Eye								
Cable								
Phone/Cell								
Internet								
Phone/Cell								
Internet								

Download free at www.universalbankingu.com

About the Author

A husband, father, grandfather, son, brother, uncle, teacher and coach, Michael Nunneley graduated from Alpena High School and Central Michigan University.

He grew up in a family-owned pharmacy business, worked for an Anheuser Busch distributor, owned his own photo center and photo studios (which got crushed when digital photography came on the scene), and served as an elected official in local politics.

Mike joined the 9th largest bank as a business banker who helped businesses with gross revenues of up to $5 MM for five years. When his bank was purchased during the Great Recession, Nunneley became a branch manager for five years. Most recently, Michael has served a credit union as a commercial lender for businesses up to ten million dollars in gross revenues and is starting a new career as a small business and technology counselor.

Nunneley currently works as a professional business advisor and lives with his wife Kim in Houghton Lake, Michigan with their dog Maverick.

Coming Soon...

10 More Financial Tips for You and Your Family

Unless You STILL HATE Your Family.

Michael Nunneley

www.ingramcontent.com/pod-product-compliance
Lightning Source LLC
Chambersburg PA
CBHW020444220526
45464CB00002B/849